BWB Texts

Short books on big subjects from
great New Zealand writers

Geering and God: 1965–71

The Heresy Trial that Divided New Zealand

LLOYD GEERING

First published as an e-book in 2013 by Bridget Williams Books Ltd,
PO Box 12474, Wellington 6144, New Zealand. Published in paperback
in 2014 by Bridget Williams Books Ltd. Reprinted 2016. The three
chapters reproduced here were first published in 2006 by Bridget
Williams Books, in association with Craig Potton Publishing, in Lloyd
Geering, *Wrestling with God: The Story of My Life*. The James K. Baxter
poem extract is used with permission.

ISBN 9781927277591 (Paperback), ISBN 9781927131930 (EPUB)
ISBN 9781927131947 (KINDLE), ISBN 9781927131954 (PDF)
ISTC A0220130000060D1

A catalogue record for this book is available from the National Library
of New Zealand. Kei te pātenga raraunga o Te Puna Mātauranga o
Aotearoa te whakarārangi o tēnei pukapuka.

Publisher: Tom Rennie
Cover and internal design: Base Two
Typesetter: Tina Delceg
Printer: Printlink, Wellington

CONTENTS

FOREWORD

The Reverend Professor Sir Lloyd Geering, ONZ, has been New Zealand's best-known teacher on religious issues for over forty-five years. Ordained in 1943, he has remained a Presbyterian minister, despite being charged with doctrinal error in 1967 in a so-called 'heresy trial' (the charges were dismissed), and his church's General Assembly in 1970 dissociating itself from his views. Ironically, the attempts to censure him gave him a much larger public platform from which to express his evolving understanding of the Christian faith and the challenges facing humanity. Honoured by his country, he has been something of a prophet without honour in the church, even reviled by some for his probing questions and the challenges he has brought to traditional Christianity.

He has been variously described as a 'prophet of modernity', 'a religious atheist', 'a Christian humanist' and a 'secular theologian', and his *Wrestling with God* (the title of his autobiography in 2006) has been a very public affair. As a teacher of Old Testament in Brisbane and Dunedin (1956–70), then as the foundation professor of religious studies at Victoria University of Wellington (1971–84), Geering moved from his deep engagement with the Hebrew world to exploring religion and humanity both historically and in the contemporary context. His sharp, incisive, logical, rational approach to exploring the meaning of the big questions, from the origins of the universe to the meaning of life and death, is seen in his clarity and ability to effectively convey complex ideas. His great contribution is not so much as an original theologian but as an interpreter of the thinking of others and its application to the modern world.

Geering's impact as a religious teacher has come through his extensive engagement both professionally and in retirement with diverse audiences through his teaching, public lecturing and writing. His university continuing education courses over many years attracted a large following. He has been a seminal speaker at Sea of Faith meetings sharing in their exploration of religious thought, and has participated in the Jesus Seminar investigating the historicity of the sayings of Jesus in the New Testament. As a columnist for the *Auckland Star* and the *New Zealand Listener*, and as a broadcaster, he brought a critical perspective to topical ethical, political and religious issues. His many books and published lectures reveal the breadth of his reading and engagement with diverse questions such as fundamentalism, ecological and environmental challenges, science and religion.

Lloyd Geering as a religious thinker stands in the inheritance of the European Enlightenment and the evolving liberal, radical approaches to the modern post-Christian secular world. The titles of some of his books – *God in the New World* (1968), *Faith's New Age* (1980), *Tomorrow's God* (1994), *The World to Come* (1999), *Christianity without God* (2002), *Coming back to Earth* (2009) – point to his continuing interests in the relationship between the world, faith, God and the future. Over time he has moved from a God who is knowable, a symbol, part of the 'process of an evolving universe', to a non-realist God – a human construct. The mystical, experiential dimensions of faith are on the periphery while scientific, rational, relativist approaches to life and faith shape his thinking.

Throughout his long life Lloyd Geering has wrestled with 'God', the deepest fundamental questions of human identity and making sense of living in this world in relationship with others. His great legacy is in provoking people to think about these questions for themselves, for the well-being of society and for the world.

Allan K. Davidson
May 2013

THRUST INTO THE LIMELIGHT...

A train of events that would soon change my life dramatically had its unobtrusive beginning in an invitation from the editor of the *Outlook* (the Presbyterian weekly) to write an article for Reformation Sunday, 31 October 1965. Taking my lead from John Robinson (who had recently published *The New Reformation?*), I confidently proceeded to discuss why such a reformation had become necessary. 'Is the Christian faith inextricably bound up with the world-view of ancient mankind, which has now been superseded,' I asked, 'or can the substance of it be translated into the world-view of twentieth century mankind?' I pointed out that, 'for the man who has stepped into the twentieth century with his eyes open, the old distinction between a natural world and a supernatural world is a thing of the past'; and that, if the church continued to ignore this fact, 'the Christian faith will continue to diminish in its influence in the world at the present alarmingly rapid rate'.

When the article appeared on 25 September, some praised it and asked for more; one reader even referred to it as 'the word of God for our age!' Others took strong exception to my rejection of the supernatural world, believing this to be an absolutely essential element of Christianity. What particularly riled the evangelicals was my blunt rejection of fundamentalism. This is what I said:

'The Bible is *not* literally inerrant. The Bible is *not* "the Word of God in written form". The Bible is *not* a simple guide setting forth what every Christian in every generation must believe and do ... [It] is a book from the ancient world and must be studied in the light of modern scholarship and all that it can tell us about the world that bequeathed to us the Bible.'

This was hardly revolutionary; after all, it had been the basis for biblical studies in seminaries for fifty years.

Early that November, my friend Jack Bates was installed as Moderator of the General Assembly, and in his Moderatorial Address he took the issue further; he hinted that any form of reformation sufficiently radical to engage the modern mind could well lead to a form of Christian atheism. No doubt he had in mind what John Robinson had said in an appendix to *The New Reformation?*:

'There is so much in the atheist's case that is true, that for many people today the only Christian faith which can be valid for them is the one that takes over after the death of God as "God" has traditionally been understood.'

Robinson then set out the atheist's case under three headings: (1) God is intellectually superfluous; (2) God is emotionally dispensable; (3) God is morally intolerable.

Robinson did not go so far as to affirm Christian atheism, but did acknowledge that he had much in common with Paul van Buren, William Hamilton and Thomas Altizer, American theologians who during 1964–65 had become known as the leading exponents of 'the death of God'. At that stage I was not more than faintly aware of their work, nor did I give them careful study until the later 1960s. Nonetheless, my critics took what I had said in my article to reflect this non-theistic position.

The most theologically able, and also the most aggressive, of my critics was the Revd Bob Blaikie. A student of the Barthian theologian Tom Torrance in Edinburgh, he had made his presence felt soon after arriving in New Zealand from Africa. After conducting a school of theology for ministers, my colleague Frank Nichol complained to me that

Bob had given him a torrid time during discussion periods. Accordingly, I had a long personal talk with Bob at the Assembly, suggesting that if he felt compelled to attack the Theological Hall staff, he should address himself to me as Principal and leave the others alone. In the light of later events, that was hardly a wise thing for me to do.

Not only did Blaikie respond to my article with a sharply critical letter in the December *Outlook,* but early in 1966 he followed it up with two articles of his own. He asserted that the kind of reformation that I (along with Robinson, Tillich, Bultmann and Bonhoeffer) had been commending was nothing less than 'the religious road to atheism' and the ultimate abandonment of Christianity altogether. He warned that the coming debate would split the church into 'the church of God and the church of the antichrist'.

This proved to be an apt forecast of things to come, for even before his articles appeared, the editor of the *Outlook* invited me in January to write an article for the Easter edition, to appear on 2 April. I had just been reading Ronald Gregor Smith's newly published book, *Secular Christianity,* and chose as the focal point of my article his challenging statement:

'... we may freely say that the bones of Jesus lie somewhere in Palestine. Christian faith is not destroyed by this admission. On the contrary, only now, when this has been said, are we in a position to ask about the meaning of the resurrection as an integral part of the message concerning Jesus.'

It had become clear to me that the question was no longer *whether or not* Jesus rose from the dead, but *what meaning* the resurrection of Jesus could possibly have within the context of our modern world-view. It could not refer to a bodily resuscitation; nor could it even be regarded as a historical event in the same way as the crucifixion. I pointed out that the New Testament itself uses a variety of ways to speak of the risen Jesus, several of which are clearly figurative and thus inconsistent with one another if taken literally. For example, Paul speaks of Christians as being 'in Christ' and thereby members of his body. The story of the empty tomb is only one of the ways of speaking of the risen Christ and should be regarded as a pious legend rather than a historical event. I suggested (no doubt having been influenced by Bultmann) that what all the stories pointed back to was the continuing influence of Jesus after his death; hence, the only way to understand his resurrection as a historical event was to recognise that 'the apostles themselves quite unexpectedly became transformed men'.

Of course, I was aware that this would come as a surprise to those readers who thought of the resurrection exclusively in terms of a resuscitated body coming forth from a tomb; and for that reason I considered toning it down. After discussing the matter fully with my wife Elaine (always my best critic) and being urged to leave it as it was, I included a warning that I had no wish to disturb the faith of those who were committed to the traditional interpretation. This discussion, I said, was for those

'... who know that the mythical three-decker universe is not the real tangible world in which we live, and because of that are genuinely puzzled to know what the modern man is to make of such an important Christian affirmation as the resurrection of Jesus.'

The storm that followed the publication of my article took me by surprise. The next issues of the *Outlook* were filled with letters to the editor – some in praise, but most in violent and angry disagreement. Additional copies of the *Outlook* were printed to meet the demand, and were accompanied by a letter from Jack Bates as Moderator of the General Assembly, who noted that 'the gap between the pulpit and pew in the understanding of the Bible has been too great for too long'. He told me on the phone that he had immediately consulted *The Manual of Doctrine* of 1950 (in the writing of which we had both been involved), and was relieved to find that it said: 'the Resurrection is not an affair of history which can be vouched for by historical tests ... and belongs to the dimension which only faith can apprehend'.

As I learned later, the editor of the *Outlook,* Peter McCallum Smith, was taken aback when he received the article and sought advice from his board as to whether he should publish it. He was a very committed Presbyterian, having been reared in the Church of Scotland, and only quite recently had considered training for the ministry himself. Understandably, he was greatly disturbed to find his journal becoming the instrument of church dissension – even though, despite some immediate cancellations, circulation numbers had increased as a result.

McCallum Smith wrote to his friend William Barclay, Professor of New Testament in his native Glasgow, to gain his opinion of the original article. Barclay replied that the article largely represented his own views, but that he would never dare say so publicly in Scotland! This seems strange, since the book by Gregor Smith that I had been quoting never caused so much as a ripple in Scotland. At any rate, Barclay's reply did little to allay McCallum Smith's continuing concern; and according to his family, he developed an agitated state that may well have contributed to his premature death the following year.

Only a few days after the Easter issue of the *Outlook* appeared, the Session of Somervell Church in Auckland unanimously expressed their conviction that my two articles constituted a radical departure from the historic Christian faith, and their resolve to protest to the Presbytery and the General Assembly. The Presbytery set up a committee to deal with the issue, and the first I heard of the protest was when its convener, Frank Winton, wrote to me, seeking clarification of my views. In answering, I pointed out that I had been writing for 'that group of people in the church who were quite keen to learn how the church interprets the Gospel in the world of the twentieth century'.

For the first six weeks, the controversy was confined to Presbyterian circles. Then the newspapers reported that the Auckland Presbytery had met in private to discuss a certain controversial article, but its members were bound to secrecy. This further attracted the interest of the press, and several newspapers then printed the offending article in full. When the *Otago Daily Times* asked a local minister why the Dunedin Presbytery hadn't even bothered to discuss the article, he replied, 'Most ministers in this city are already familiar with these theories of the resurrection because they read their theological journals'.

The *Otago Daily Times* followed this with an editorial, quoting Dean Raphael of the Dunedin Cathedral; he had not only preached in support of the article, but reported what his own office-bearer had said to him afterwards: 'That is what we lay people have privately thought for a long time but kept quiet about for fear of offending the clergy'. Thus, what started as a Presbyterian debate quickly became a public one. Anglicans, Catholics and others joined Presbyterians in making public statements, both in favour and in protest. Even secular journalists of the press and radio joined in, discussing at considerable length what they thought about the reports of Jesus' resurrection from the dead.

In a very short time I found myself the centre of public attention, a situation for which I was ill prepared. I was not used to being interviewed and questioned by journalists from the press, radio and television, and not accustomed to seeing my name in the paper nearly every day, usually as the butt of attack and bitter criticism. It may be a very pleasant experience to become suddenly famous, but to be the subject of public notoriety is altogether different.

All this brought about a sudden change in my reading habits. I began to read so vigorously that my reading speed accelerated rapidly and has remained at that level ever since. My record of the books I was reading shows a sudden shift of interest away from the Old Testament, which had naturally taken up most of my reading time until then. First, I read everything I could find on the resurrection of Jesus, including a book by Hans Grass that has never been translated into English. I felt compelled to reassure myself that I had not overstepped the mark, and nearly everything I read confirmed in one way or another all that I had said.

On my own shelves was a commentary on Mark's Gospel which I had bought in 1942 but not yet read. Its author was Henry Major, who after theological training and parish ministry in New Zealand had gone to Oxford for further study and become the leading Anglican modernist in England. After discussing the three possible ways in which 'resurrection' could be conceived, Major concluded that, to make any sense for the modern mind,

'... the mode of the Resurrection must be psychological and subjective. The belief in the Resurrection of Jesus was created ... by the impact of His personality upon the personality of the disciples in the preceding period.'

Hans Lietzman, the celebrated church historian whose books Helmut Rex had encouraged me to read, had likewise argued in 1937 that all attempts to discover the facts behind the Gospel narratives had to be carried out on the basis of our own experience of the way things happen. As he put it, 'the true nature of the event described as the resurrection of Jesus does not come within the province of historical enquiry into matters of fact; it belongs to the place where the human soul touches the eternal'. In short, all my research showed me to be fully in tune with the conclusions of much of the scholarly world, even if not with public sentiment in New Zealand.

I began to receive hundreds of letters, and replied to as many of them as time allowed. Both friends and strangers in great numbers offered support and told me that a burden had been lifted from their shoulders. That this was a common theme in letters I received throughout the next two years showed how many people had been trying to be faithful to their church despite the difficulty of reconciling traditional doctrine with modern knowledge.

Other letters were strongly critical, some going so far as to accuse me of being the agent of the devil. On 2 June I received the following telegram:

'YOU HAVE CAUSED UNTOLD PAIN AND DOUBTS BY THE STATEMENTS AS TO YOUR POSITION. MY WIFE HAS JUST GOT OVER A NERVOUS BREAKDOWN AND A RELAPSE IS POSSIBLE. I CHALLENGE YOU TO PUBLIC [SIC] DEBATE YOUR VIEW WITH ME. I AM A BARRISTER OF THE SUPREME COURT WITH OVER THIRTY-FIVE YEARS EXPERIENCE. PLEASE REPLY URGENTLY.'

Were my words as damaging to people's health as this implied? I respectfully declined the invitation, on the grounds that public debating of that kind 'neither nurtures faith nor determines historical facts but merely confirms prejudices'.

At first I tried to respond to each letter personally, but the vast number appearing in the *Outlook* alone made this impossible. In an attempt to pour oil on troubled waters, I decided to write four more articles for the *Outlook,* explaining the background to the controversy. More than a little shocked by the sudden furore, I wanted to disabuse people of the unfortunate notion that I had set out to sow dissension. At the suggestion of the editor, I prefaced the articles with this general reply to those who had written:

'My brothers and sisters in Christ, if this article contains some plain speaking, I am even more concerned to try and ensure that I am speaking the truth in love. No personal offence is in any way intended. I have welcomed your letters and take no offence from anything you have said, for I do not doubt for one moment you are absolutely sincere. We must all agree that there is no place for bitterness and personal recriminations among Christians. We are here to witness to the truth as we understand it, and to help one another embrace it.'

I naively supposed that once people were brought up to date on current theological thinking, they would soon come to see everything in a different light.

In the first article, 'Knowledge or Faith? That Is the Question', I distinguished between knowledge (which is open to critical enquiry) and faith (which is an attitude of trust). Faith is not a matter of accepting uncritically a set of beliefs, I said, quoting one of my favourite authors. The nineteenth-century clergyman C. L. Dodgson, better known as Lewis Carroll, used *Alice in Wonderland* to make fun of people who accepted beliefs uncritically. There we find, for instance, that when Alice says she cannot believe impossible things, the White Queen urges her to practise it for half-an-hour a day, adding, 'Sometimes I've believed as many as six impossible things before breakfast'.

In the second article, 'The Empty Tomb', I showed that the historicity of the empty tomb story had not been confirmed by any secular historian. I then quoted a series of biblical scholars and theologians – including Alfred von Harnack, James Denny, Kirsopp Lake, Karl Barth and Emil Brunner – all of whom declared that faith in the resurrection of Jesus did not depend on the historicity of the empty tomb story.

The third article was titled 'The Westminster Confession – Our Master or Our Servant?' It was aimed at those who contended that, as a Presbyterian minister, I was bound by my ordination vows to remain faithful to the beliefs expressed in the Westminster Confession. After sketching the origin and purpose of the Westminster documents, I showed how Presbyterian churches throughout the world had, for more than sixty years, been uneasy about these subordinate standards, regarding them as no longer relevant to the modern world. Indeed, the meeting of Presbyterian theologians I had attended in Germany in 1964 had declared the continuing role of the Westminster Confession to be a dead issue.

In the final article, 'The Word of God and the Bible', I outlined how the nineteenth century had witnessed a revolution in the way we understand the Bible. I distinguished between the literal reading of Holy Scripture and the hearing of the Word of God, the latter being a personal and subjective experience. I also quoted Dean Farrar, who said in 1886, 'Whoever was the first dogmatist to make the terms "the Bible" and "the word of God" synonymous rendered to the cause of truth and of religion an immense disservice'.

These articles seemed to me at the time – as they still do today – to answer all the objections that my critics had raised. Further, they showed that I was not the isolated maverick I was being made out to be, for Christian scholars elsewhere offered wide support for everything I had said. But far from having the desired effect, my articles were like petrol thrown on an already blazing fire.

From the beginning I was loyally supported by

the staff at the Theological Hall, who decided to offer an opportunity for public questioning and discussion. Some three hundred people packed into the hall at Knox College to hear us speak and answer their questions. It was an opportunity to show our solidarity, and at the same time to indicate that there was room for different viewpoints. The staff of the (Catholic) Holy Cross College arranged a similar event, but one with different results, for although open to the public its primary aim was to reassure Catholics. We were informed, for example, that Catholics believe there are three 'bodies' residing in heaven: Elijah (having been taken up in a whirlwind), Jesus (having risen and ascended), and the Virgin Mary (by virtue of the dogma of her bodily assumption).

Even the poet James K. Baxter became involved, having by that time become a Catholic. Then a Burns Fellow at the University of Otago, he wrote a poem for the student journal *Critic*, which began:

> I'm feeling ecumenical
> And yet it saddens me
> To learn that Dr Geering
> Sincerely cannot see
> That resurrection would require
> A resurrected body.

I wrote an anonymous reply, and to this day few people know who was responsible for what appeared in the next issue of *Critic*. I include it here as a little light relief, for to my surprise it was recently included in an anthology of New Zealand spiritual verse, *Spirit in a Strange Land*.

> To a James K. Baxter – Celestial Greeting!
> What joy there'll be at our future meeting.
> The 'Critic' was left by a student of late
> In the waiting-room at the pearly gate.
> I began to read it when traffic was slow,
> And espied your poem – jolly good show!
> I passed it around and we all agreed,
> That for pleas of this kind there's an urgent need.
> Too few in these days have enough concern
> As to whether in future they'll harp or burn.
> Your keen request is received and noted,
> And ready in future to be re-quoted.
> But just one warning I'm bidden to give –
> You can bear it in mind on earth as you live:
> My good friend Paul, you may have read,
> Once wrote to Corinth, and there he said,
> That flesh and blood can never inherit
> The Kingdom intended for those of merit.
> That body of dust you must leave behind.
> There's a spiritual body here you'll find.
> How else do you think, for all this time,
> I've wielded the keys and writ this rime?
> For surely you know my bones still lie
> In the city of Rome, the Tiber nigh.
> This spiritual body I find much neater,
> Yours truly, Cephas (Known as St Peter).

What became ever clearer, as the controversy dragged on in the press and in the church courts, was that widespread ignorance existed in both the churches and the general public regarding the radical changes that had been taking place in biblical scholarship and Christian thought in the previous hundred years. Much of what had been taught in the seminaries for decades had never reached the people in the pews, let alone the public at large. This was partly because many ministers, afraid of causing dissension in their congregations, were reluctant to share with them the new understanding of the Bible, which even the ministers themselves may have found disturbing at first. As a result, it was still widely assumed that everything in the Bible was to be taken literally.

During these months, the material appearing in newspapers was mounting rapidly. It is quite by accident that I have much of it now preserved. In 1965, well before any hint appeared of the coming controversy, the staff at the Theological Hall had been discussing whether to subscribe to a professional news-clipping service. When we finally decided it was too expensive, I resolved to undertake the project myself, though on a smaller scale. I had no sooner started than the public uproar began.

A British New Testament scholar, Dr A. R. C. Leaney, was then visiting New Zealand to lecture at

St John's College in Auckland. This seemed a good opportunity for people to hear an alternative view on the resurrection from an authoritative source, so he and I were invited to engage in a televised discussion. To be sure, he was somewhat more conservative than I, and did his best to defend the more traditional view of the resurrection; but after the programme, he admitted to me privately that the traditional view did not altogether stand up. Leaney was also invited to write an article for the *Outlook*. Being the kindly person he was, Leaney was careful not to contradict anything I had said; he did not even mention the 'empty tomb', but traced the belief in the resurrection to the so-called 'appearances' to the disciples. Thus he did not bring much comfort to my critics. Then, just prior to the General Assembly, the church published my five articles in booklet form, along with Leaney's article and another by my colleague Evan Pollard.

Two other British scholars visited New Zealand at this time, and the press immediately asked them for their views. Hugh Montefiore, then Canon of Coventry but later Bishop of Birmingham, said that he agreed with me; but F. F. Bruce, Professor of Biblical Criticism at Manchester, with a background in the Brethren, declared that 'bodily resurrection is the only sense that could have been intended by the first preachers and understood by the first hearers'. He went on to say that I had set out to make people think and had certainly succeeded, but that the Bible would withstand any test of that kind.

In the meantime, as the controversy continued with deadly seriousness and at times much heat, Sir James Fletcher and Sir William Goodfellow sponsored a public meeting of Presbyterian laymen. Seventeen hundred people gathered in the Auckland Town Hall and called for a New Zealand Association of Presbyterian Laymen (NZAPL) to be established for the express purpose of restoring sound doctrine to the Presbyterian Church. A representative gathering of 120 laymen eventually approved a constitution (which provided for women to be admitted only as associate members) and elected R. J. Wardlaw of Auckland as the national chairman. The NZAPL then began a widespread advertising campaign (Wardlaw ran an advertising firm) and held meetings throughout the country. Seven hundred people filled the Dunedin Concert Chamber, but a subsequent meeting in Invercargill ended in disorder, for the association was itself coming under severe criticism for potentially causing a split within the church.

Public advertisements for the NZAPL prompted the 'Gallery' current affairs programme to invite Bob Wardlaw and me to be interviewed by Austin Mitchell and Graham Billing. The whole exercise gave me a valuable insight into how television can manipulate people. The show was pre-recorded, and when the director decided that Bob and I had been too 'nice' to each other, he made a second recording after instructing us to be much more aggressive. Accordingly, I challenged Bob on a number of points, but later felt very bad about it, as my normal approach in theological debate was to be as conciliatory as possible within the limits of integrity. Of the thirty-four letters I received as a result of the programme, eleven were critical and twenty-three were supportive.

Following this debate, the Auckland Church of Christ (not to be confused with the Associated Churches of Christ) placed a full-page advertisement in the *New Zealand Herald,* entitled 'Was Prof. Geering right on TV?' One of its many headlines asserted, 'Heaven *is* a place, Professor Geering!' (To demonstrate how far we have moved in just over thirty years, in 1999 no less an authority than Pope John Paul II made headlines in *The Times* of London by saying, 'Heaven is *not* a place. It is a state of mind.')

While denying it was an attack on me personally, the *Herald* advertisement stated that it had been inserted in support of 'Bible-believing Christians in the Presbyterian Church'; it also cited biblical passages to show that many of the things I had said on television were in direct conflict with statements found in the Bible. This was true, of course; and it characterises a line of argument that appears to give the fundamentalists the high moral ground. Unfortunately, they conveniently ignore the fact that the Bible, being an anthology of books written by different people in different times and cultural contexts, is far from being consistent.

The national conference of the NZAPL, held in early October, decided to circulate a petition in the press, inviting public support. The petition sought the coming General Assembly to reaffirm: (a) the supernatural nature of the Person of God, (b) the deity of Jesus Christ His Son, and (c) the fact of the resurrection of Christ in true, real, visible and tangible form. It also asked the General Assembly to rule that doctrines opposed to these should not be taught in the church's theological college.

In the meantime, a proposal was brought before the Auckland Presbytery calling for the resignation of all Theological Hall staff members whose thinking was incompatible with biblical faith. Although this was defeated, my long-time critic Bob Blaikie (who denied any connection with the newly formed NZAPL) succeeded in having forwarded to the Assembly an overture calling for reaffirmation of the basic Christian doctrines. This was only one of several such initiatives sent to the Assembly.

The Doctrine Committee of the Presbyterian Church had decided at its annual August meeting not to take up time in discussing my articles, as they were not published as official statements. By October, however, it was forced by the increasing tension within the church to have something ready for the coming General Assembly in an attempt to restore confidence. As Principal, I was *ex officio* a member of the Doctrine Committee, but was prevented from saying a word during its deliberations. This resulted not from any ecclesiastical restraint, but from a bad attack of laryngitis which left me completely speechless. Some judged this to be an act of God!

What the Doctrine Committee did was to assemble evidence from the biblical material to support the affirmation that Jesus rose from the dead. To my dismay, it ignored much of the scholarly work that I had so recently canvassed. What I would have said, had I been able, was that they had entirely missed the point of my original article. It had not been my concern to deny what the committee was so anxious to reaffirm – namely, that *according to the New Testament* 'Jesus rose from the dead'. Clearly, this is what the New Testament states. The problem was this: the New Testament writers believed that they lived in a three-decker universe, consisting of heaven, earth and the underworld of the dead. Within that framework of belief, to say that Jesus rose (from the underworld of the dead) and 'ascended into heaven' made sense; for us, who see ourselves living in a space-time universe, it does not.

Even the Doctrine Committee had difficulty finding the words that would satisfy all its members, a clear indication that this was a topic on which they had a variety of views. Changes were being made to their statement right up until the morning of the Assembly, after which it was to be presented as an addendum to their annual report.

The 1966 General Assembly met in St John's Church, Wellington, in an atmosphere of tense expectancy. The newly installed Moderator was Stan Read of St Andrew's Church, Wellington, whom I had known personally ever since he officiated at the funeral of my brother Ira in 1939. That I was well known to so many of the leading ministers of the church unfortunately led many of my critics, particularly those of the laity, to assume that the support I received sprang from friendship rather than theological conviction, and that consequently they were not receiving a fair hearing.

Stan Read, however, tried to be strictly neutral, and in his opening address set the stage for the coming debate. On the one hand, he said that some contemporary theologians who attempted to relate the Christian message to the modern age were 'like the housewife who used nitric acid to take a stain off her tablecloth. It took away both the stain and the cloth'. (It was not clear whether he was referring to me or not.) On the other hand, he called upon parish ministers to have done with 'moralistic waffling' and 'pious blather', and to grapple with the problem of relating the Christian message to modern life. He called for 'an aggressive evangelism which, though Bible based, was directed to secular man'. He pointed out that the secular world was rooted in the Gospel and in biblical ideals stemming from the Israelite prophets.

This augured well for a good debate, and the church was packed to overflowing to hear it. But first, five overtures from presbyteries and sessions had to be received. Then Bob Wardlaw, in presenting a petition signed by nearly five thousand people, aroused considerable anger when he referred to the 'odd-ball college of theology'. Later the Revd Hemi Potatau, Moderator of the Presbyterian Maori Synod, received warm applause for his description of visits to the holy Christian sites in Palestine while serving in the Maori Battalion, and concluded by saying that if the Assembly did not accept the bodily resurrection of Christ, he wanted to become a savage again. Others spoke of people leaving the church as a result of its uncertainty on basic issues.

The debate lasted seven hours, during which laymen repeatedly asked for simple, easily understood declarations of faith instead of the complex theological language being used by the scholars. Eventually, after many amendments had been moved, a few accepted, and many rejected, the statement prepared by the Doctrine Committee was approved by an overwhelming majority. It said, among other things, that 'God raised Jesus Christ from the dead in triumph over sin and death to reign with the Father as sovereign over all'. This drew upon such traditional language that neither liberal nor conservative could disagree with it, simply because it fudged the issues that had been raised. It neither distinguished between theological statements and historical statements, nor addressed the question of what was meant by 'resurrection from the dead'. And that is what the controversy was really about.

Nevertheless, there was great rejoicing that the imminent split in the church had been averted, and Bob Wardlaw greeted the result as a partial victory. The Assembly then agreed on a Message to the Church, summarising the statement on the resurrection and instructing this to be read from every Presbyterian pulpit.

The Clerk of the South Auckland Presbytery announced that it was withdrawing its overture, which among other things had called for the establishment of a second, conservative theological college. This was the opportunity for the Theological Education Committee to present a statement on the 'Aims and Methods of Theological Education', in an attempt to make clear to lay people how it trained students for the ministry. At that point,

I spoke for the first time in the Assembly. I said, among other things, 'Apart from the conjugation of Hebrew verbs (which allowed no variation from the established norm) we shun indoctrination of any kind and encourage students to reach their own mature convictions'. Somewhat to my surprise, my short burst was met with warm applause. In reporting the Assembly debate, the *Evening Post* noted with some humour that when People's Night of the Assembly was held in the Wellington Town Hall, the combined choirs appropriately sang 'God has gone up' and 'The strife is o'er'.

The Governor-General of New Zealand, Sir Bernard Fergusson, had been invited to address the Assembly. Being a staunch Presbyterian from the Church of Scotland, he was very interested in the theological debate that had become the focus of the Assembly's discussions. Although he carefully avoided taking sides, he did refer to it in his remarks. Then he sent me a private message inviting me to Government House that evening to explain the issue to him over a glass of sherry.

The Assembly's decision would have been the end of the matter (as many people hoped), had it been a genuine and honest resolution. In fact, it had simply papered over the cracks with traditional yet ambiguous statements, in an attempt to restore church harmony. Few in the church were willing to face up to the reality of the theological problems that had given rise to the controversy and remained unresolved. Events were soon to show the hollowness of the unanimity that had been reached.

Still, it is doubtful whether the Assembly could have done anything else, for the floor of the Assembly is not the place to decide complex theological issues. I remember John Dickie once observing that most Christians were happy to accept the historic creeds, largely because of the authority of ancient tradition and rhetoric, yet they would never be able to agree on a credal formula articulated in modern language. We have to remember that not even the ecumenical councils of the early centuries were unanimous when they settled on the historic creeds; these *appeared* to be universal only because the vigorous minority that disagreed with them were eased out of the 'one holy catholic church'. In other words, the original creeds had been arrived at *only by causing a split among Christians,* an extremity that the Presbyterian Church of New Zealand had avoided – at least for the time being.

As 1966 drew to a close, I hoped that life would return to normal. The pressures of this public debate had made increasing demands on my time, over and above my regular duties in the Hall and at home, which naturally continued as usual. Certainly there had been less time for leisure pursuits, though I seem to recall remaining one of the friendly four golfers who went around the Ocean Beach Links on Monday afternoons. All of our children were still at home and, apart from a few quite normal adolescent problems, family life proceeded very smoothly and seemed little, if at all, affected by the limelight now being directed our way.

...AND CHARGED WITH HERESY

The unanimity of the 1966 Assembly decision on the 'resurrection controversy' seemed to provide a climate in which theological discussion could proceed in a more relaxed style. Indeed, 1967 began in a semblance of theological calm which allowed occasional titbits of humorous exchange. An open letter to me appeared in the *Manawatu Times,* composed entirely of passages from the Pauline epistles by someone who signed himself 'Paul'. Naturally he included the words 'If Christ was not raised then neither our preaching nor your faith has any meaning at all'. The very next day came the following reply:

'Sir, I am most annoyed that it has been necessary for me to interrupt my harp lessons to correspond with you in this barbarous English tongue, but a letter in yesterday's edition, delivered up here by special arrangement, leaves me no choice. How dare one of your citizens call himself by my name – "Paul". As if I had not had enough of this apocryphal use of my name in the first five centuries of this era!

How dare he throw chunks of my writings at your readers, out of context, to make me seem to say what I have no intention of saying. The Risen Christ I met on the Damascus Road was certainly not flesh and blood nor is my description of the after-life suggestive that we retain a physical form of life "up here".

I have not met this fellow Geering (although he has made long-term reservations here) but he seems to be aware of the Risen Christ's presence in the world in much the same way as I knew him there.

Please see that there is no nonsense about adding this letter to the Canon. – Yours, etc., "Saint" (If you please) Paul.'

But this more relaxed atmosphere was soon to be shattered once again. John Murray, then ecumenical chaplain at Victoria University of Wellington, had invited me to preach at the annual inaugural university service in March. I chose to speak about the Book of Ecclesiastes, for I saw in this book reflections of many contemporary problems. After all, it had been written by a Jewish thinker who was struggling to resolve the conflict between his religious heritage and the cultural context of Hellenistic Alexandria.

Noting that we lived in a similarly unsettling

environment, I pointed out that we had already accepted many aspects of today's secular culture, even when they conflicted with traditional Christian doctrines. For example, the human sciences had concluded that 'Man is a psychosomatic creature whose psyche cannot live independently from his body. Man has no immortal soul.' Yet such a revelation, I showed, simply took us back to Ecclesiastes and even to the early Christians, for they also accepted their mortality, as we now had to do. The remarkable thing about the human condition, I continued, and that which separated us from the other animals, was not that we are immortal but that, as Ecclesiastes states, 'God has put eternity into our minds'. In other words, 'We know we must die. Yet we have glimpses of the whole human situation – of the vast universe – of time – and beyond that again of the mystery of God.'

Unlike many sermons of mine and of others, this one has stood the test of time surprisingly well. I delivered it recently without having to change a word, and in it discovered the seeds of many ideas I was later to develop in my books. I said, for example, 'There are sound theological and historical reasons why secular man has emerged out of the Judeo-Christian heritage and not from elsewhere. The Christian can welcome the birth of secular culture.'

However, when an enterprising (and religiously conservative) journalist in the congregation heard me deliver the sermon in 1967, he seized upon the words, 'Man has no immortal soul', seeing it as another radical departure from orthodoxy on my part. After it had been headlined in the next morning's news, he then telephoned various church leaders to ask them what they thought. Most appeared shocked.

Three days later, the president of the Association of Presbyterian Laymen, Bob Wardlaw, called for my immediate resignation or, failing that, my dismissal. He even wrote to evangelical students in the Theological Hall, urging them to boycott my lectures. A contrary editorial in the *Otago Daily Times* warned Presbyterians 'to consider very carefully before they think of rushing to Mr Wardlaw's support in a personal witch-hunt'. And I received further support from a most unexpected source. When addressing a conference of students at Victoria University, the Minister of Labour, the Hon. T. P. Shand, discussed my case at some length and concluded that I should be accorded academic freedom and not dismissed from my post.

As a result of Wardlaw's protest, my sermon was subsequently published in most newspapers; this was followed by widespread public discussion on the sensitive issue of what happens to us when we die. A full-page feature in the very next *Sunday News* quoted authorities from around the world and manifested conflicting views. The Anglican

Bishop of Auckland asserted that to deny life after death was to deny the teaching of Jesus Christ. The Roman Catholic hierarchy, in a statement to reassure their faithful, asserted that 'The eternal God who makes man to his own image or likeness means him to live for ever ... To reject this belief is to reduce man to the level of a mere animal'.

It so happened that in the previous December the Mataura Presbytery had invited me, along with Ian Breward, to discuss all the issues of the 1966 controversy at a full-day seminar open to all the lay people in Gore. To be sure, the decision to invite us had not been reached without some opposition; some in Gore would have preferred that I not be one of the two Hall staff members invited. Nevertheless, it was a more constructive way of proceeding.

Since the day chosen for the seminar turned out to be the Saturday following the outbreak of this second controversy, the atmosphere was once again very tense. Although only Presbyterians were admitted, the event drew an audience of two hundred. With two lectures apiece, Ian Breward and I had an excellent opportunity to explain theological education in general, and in particular to outline the extent and significance of the previous hundred years of revolution in our understanding of the Bible.

The press were not admitted, but were permitted to publish selected transcripts of our answers to questions we were asked, many of which naturally arose from the new controversy then emerging. For example, on being asked about the meaning of eternal life, I distinguished between it and 'life after death', declaring the latter phrase to be a contradiction in terms, since death is what brings life to an end. Death has to be taken seriously, I said, and that is why Christian theologians have never used the phrase 'life after death'. The Christian term 'eternal life' refers to the quality of life that can be experienced here and now, a quality that enables us to face both life and death with a serenity and sense of victory that take the sting out of the universal phenomenon of death.

I even dared to illustrate our ambivalence with regard to the popular view of 'life after death' by telling the story of a minister who was visiting his former parish. On meeting an old parishioner, Mrs Smith, he immediately enquired after Mr Smith, only to be told, 'Mr Smith is in heaven'. Without thinking he replied, 'I'm so sorry to hear that', only to realise that was not an appropriate response. Correcting himself, he blurted, 'I'm glad to know that', but immediately recognised that he had moved into even deeper waters. In desperation, he made one last attempt to salvage the situation by saying, 'I *am* surprised'.

On the day after the seminar, I preached in the leading Presbyterian church in Gore, and my sermon was published almost in full in the following Saturday's newspaper. I spoke about faith, distinguishing it from knowledge and orthodox doctrine. Faith, I said, is an attitude of trust in the face of both doubt and uncertainty. 'Unless you experience some doubt, you don't know what faith is. The person who believes he possesses an infallible Bible does not need to live by faith.'

The whole weekend proved very successful, particularly since Gore, along with Southland generally, was known to be a conservative area. Although not everyone agreed with our honest answers to their questions, this valuable educational and pastoral exercise demonstrated that it was far better to discuss these delicate and controversial issues face to face than to hurl invectives from a distance.

It is a great pity that this seminar did not become the prototype for many more. Instead, a largely impersonal debate continued in the public arena and mainly through the media. The New Zealand Rationalist Association offered £1,000 to anyone who could provide scientific proof that human beings possessed immortal souls. The ultra-conservative Churches of Christ offered £5,000 to the first person to produce one clear instance of the term 'immortal soul' in the Bible. Neither amount was claimed.

Day after day the newspapers carried letters

to the editor, reports of presbytery meetings, and articles on immortality by all and sundry. It is doubtful whether, at any other time, so many people in New Zealand were all thinking about the question of 'life after death'. It was such a talking point that the British Secretary of the Bible Society, on arriving in New Zealand, was immediately asked by the media whether he believed in the immortality of the soul. 'Indeed I do,' he said, 'I see no point whatever in this life if when we die we are dead and finished with.' When news of the debate reached Australia, the *Sydney Morning Herald* devoted an editorial to it and followed that up with a full-page article in its *Weekend Magazine* on whether we humans have immortal souls.

Arthur Gunn, Moderator of the South Auckland Presbytery and the leading light of the conservative Westminster Fellowship, attempted to show that I had clearly stepped outside the boundaries of allowable Presbyterian thinking. His strategy was to call the public's attention to the relevant words in the Westminster Confession, which ministers and teachers of the church were bound to uphold. But as early as 1940 John Dickie had pointed out to us students that the complicated eschatology enshrined in the Westminster Confession was based on two mutually exclusive and hence contradictory views. One – a doctrine that became dominant in the Middle Ages – was that the eternal destiny of the soul was determined immediately after death. The other was that the dead sleep in their graves until the end of the world, at which point they are resurrected to appear before the Judgement seat of God. This, he said, was the original view of both Jews and Christians, and it showed the influence of Persian religion. That is why the earliest Christian epitaph was *Requiescat in pace* (let him or her rest in peace). This second view was revived by Martin Luther but rejected by John Calvin, who scathingly condemned the notion of 'soul-sleep'.

During the gathering controversy I received a phone call from a ninety-year-old Presbyterian minister, who said, 'I cannot understand what all the fuss is about. I have been going back to my old copies of the *Outlook* that I have kept from my young days and I find that all these issues were being discussed then.' He was referring to the fact that the influential minister Rutherford Waddell had said in 1897, 'The idea of immortality as something to come ... which still lingers on in many minds, is really a survival of paganism'. Thus he illustrated a perennial problem of new theological thinking: it is all too soon forgotten as a new generation arises, one that 'knows not Joseph'.

The widespread public interest in the topic caused feelings within the church to become very strained. The Moderator of the General Assembly, S. C. (Stan) Read, asked Presbyterians not to be thrown into a state of panic. As Easter drew near, I was informed that a deputation led by the Moderator was coming to see me on Thursday of Holy Week. Although unclear as to what the deputation hoped to achieve, I assumed that they wished to discuss the issues I had raised and perhaps ask me to recant. Convinced that I had no reason to retract anything I had said, I had my books ready and open to show them that it had already been said by scholars of international repute. When they said that was not their mission, I asked if they wished me to resign, indicating that I was willing to do so, however reluctantly, if it was necessary to restore harmony in the church. Again they said that was not what they sought. Rather, they asked me to do all in my power to prevent the controversy from hurting the church. This I happily agreed to, pointing out, however, that if the church did not face up honestly to issues I had raised, it would have no future.

I learned later from Evan Sherrard (who, although a recent student, had been invited to join the delegation at the last moment) that the visit had been motivated by a pastoral concern both for me and for the church, and that I was in no sense 'on trial'. All in all, the meeting was very unsatisfactory and resolved nothing, partly because I had felt so much on the defensive as to persuade the deputation that I was not open to dialogue. On their way out, the group passed my colleague

Frank Nichol, who commented with a wicked smile, 'My! This must be some funeral you're planning!' And that was the feeling I was left with, for the significance of the day – Maundy Thursday – did not escape me. I went home to drive the family up to our cottage at Cromwell for the Easter break. And a very bleak Easter it was, for this was the one time throughout the entire controversy when I felt isolated from the whole of the church.

From that time onwards, I found myself increasingly singled out as the cause of widespread dissension. It was being called 'the Geering affair'. What should have been a worthwhile theological discussion, providing a number of positive outcomes, became instead a debate centred on me, as if I bore sole responsibility for the disturbance by suddenly making some outrageous claims that no one else had ever thought of.

That Easter Day, a well-known ninety-year-old New Zealander wrote to tell me that his belief in an after-life had been his sheet anchor since the death of his wife twenty-eight years before. He implied that it was his expectation of meeting her again that had enabled him to live to such a great age. There seemed to be something illogical here, for if one is so convinced of such a reunion, one would hardly take such delight in living a long life. Indeed, a few people have been known to take their own lives in order to be quickly reunited with those they love.

Of course, I replied to this man as sympathetically as I could (as I did with the rest of the deluge of letters I received), even though I concurred with Paul Tillich that ministers ought to steer people away from the hope of being reunited with their loved ones in the hereafter.

In early April my colleague Frank Nichol, Professor of Systematic Theology, and my parish minister, Rod Madill, came to my support by bringing motions to the Dunedin Presbytery. After lengthy debate, the Presbytery went so far as to congratulate me on the sermon on Ecclesiastes, urged people to study it in full, and deplored the way in which words had been taken out of context to accuse me of theological error.

Although I always enjoyed warm support from my colleagues, most of the students, and those who knew me in Dunedin, the further I departed from 'home' the more uncertain I became of what to expect. At times the antagonism was not only highly personal, but also quite vicious. Some of my critics prophesied that God's curse would descend upon me in the form of fire and brimstone or some equally excruciating commodity. When death threats started to arrive, my advisers insisted that I inform the police. This I reluctantly did, and although I was offered police protection, I deemed it unnecessary. Rather than fearful, I felt staggered and ashamed that those who prided themselves on being Christian could harbour such vicious thoughts and motives.

And I was not the only target. In many ways my family suffered more than I did, for they had done nothing and were unable to defend themselves. Elaine fielded many abusive phone calls, unwelcome objects were sent through the post, and our children found that their peers could sometimes be unexpectedly cruel.

The intensely personal nature of the controversy made it clear to me that not only in the church but in society at large a very sensitive nerve had been touched. I happened to be the person who triggered the response, but it could have been any one of a large number of people. I found myself being referred to in the most extreme terms, as everything from the devil incarnate to the new Galileo. In most of this I was quite unable to recognise myself: it seemed as if a new mental image of me had formed in the collective consciousness of New Zealanders – an image that some hated and others honoured. The Christian tradition was clearly at a fork in the road. A fault-line had long been developing between traditional and popular Christian thought on the one hand, and academic enquiry on the other; now the fracture zone had become a yawning gulf.

In the midst of this intense public turmoil I was invited by the staff of Canterbury University to participate in an evening of theological discussion.

On arrival in Christchurch I found I was expected to give an address, and was obliged to spend an hour or two putting my hastily prepared notes into better shape. That evening I spoke to an overflowing university hall on 'Man's Ultimate Destiny'. In the Victoria University sermon that had sparked the new commotion, I had been primarily concerned to show the relevance of the Christian tradition to a rapidly changing world. Here now was an opportunity to discuss at some length the topic of human destiny, which people had wrongly assumed to have been the point of the sermon.

First, I drew attention to the fact that all cultures and religions had evolved in order to answer the basic questions we ask about human existence, and that each of them had developed and matured over the centuries. To show the changes in the Judeo-Christian tradition, I then selected three historical cross-sections. In the first, portrayed in the Old Testament, humans accepted their personal mortality and believed their appointed role was to contribute to the ongoing destiny of their people, Israel. In the second, the period of Christian origins, human destiny was described in terms of salvation from the present evil age and the transition to a new age, the coming of a new heaven and a new earth. When that promised world failed to arrive, the third dispensation, which corresponded with the medieval period, came to picture the ultimate human destiny as a supernatural spiritual heaven, to be entered after death.

All three cross-sections were part of our cultural past, I said, but none of them was adequate in today's world, although the first had best stood the test of time. I concluded with some suggestions as to the most satisfying answer to the meaning of existence in today's world. The most important of these, I proposed, was that we must accept our mortality and acknowledge that all we valued in life was bound up with our bodies and the bodies of others.

'All thought of immortal souls, life after death, heavenly existence are but pale shadows in comparison. The life we have here, with all its frustrations and finiteness, is capable of maturing to the best that we actually imagine, and that is the meaning of the Christian doctrine of the incarnation.'

My lecture was received with great applause, and I felt flattered when the chairman judged it to be indicative of genuine creative thinking.

I have included this brief sketch for two reasons. First, like the sermon at Victoria University, it has stood the test of time rather well and contains the germ of much that I was to develop later. The second is that it had more immediate consequences. Having promised the Moderator not to be the cause of further dissension in the church, I had agreed to accept the invitation only on the condition that the audience would be restricted to members of the university, and that no one was to record what was said. Although the chairman made this clear at the outset, someone not only recorded the lecture but passed the audiotape on to my accusers, with consequences that will be discussed later.

Recognising that the controversy revealed great confusion in the public mind about central theological issues, I accepted an invitation to write a book about them. In fact, I was approached by three publishers, but responded only to Hodder & Stoughton, who had been the first to contact me late in 1966. As I had never imagined myself as an author, I felt such a novice that at first I submitted a few chapters for their approval. It seemed to me necessary to leave aside the topics of resurrection and immortality for the time being, so as to explain in non-academic language what lay behind the current controversy. Thus during the first eight months of 1967, while the theological storm was swirling around me, I was producing a chapter every fortnight – although towards the end a note of urgency crept in when I realised the book would have to be finished before the meeting of the General Assembly. That is how I came to write *God in the New World*.

Just after beginning the book, I read with excitement *The Phenomenon of Man*, the magnum opus of the Jesuit scientist Teilhard de Chardin. I read it over one weekend, hardly putting it down. Here was a vision of the evolving universe, one that put all that we have come to know about cosmology, physics, chemistry and biology into one developing story. I was awestruck. This visionary sketch of a vast, immemorial process that eventually produced the human species was a more convincing description of God than Tillich's enigmatic phrase 'being itself'. God is not so much the maker of the world, the first cause or even the planner of the evolutionary process; rather, the mysterious process of an evolving universe is itself God. It is little wonder that the then popular 'process theology', originating with the philosopher A. N. Whitehead, came to be seen as consistent with Teilhard's vision.

Unbeknown to me, during these months a good deal of correspondence about my future was going on up and down the country, particularly between the Association of Presbyterian Laymen and the Moderator. The former, having failed to achieve my immediate dismissal, had called for a special meeting of the General Assembly to be held forthwith. This request was eventually declined, and it was left to the normal meeting of the Assembly in November to deal with the issue.

In view of what had happened the year before, it is understandable that the NZAPL should have reacted as strongly as it did. But curiously enough, they did not realise that on this issue they could not call on the Bible for support, as they could with regard to the resurrection, for the New Testament unambiguously declares that only God is immortal. All this was made clear in a book I had read in 1959, *The Immortality of the Soul or the Resurrection of the Dead?* by Oscar Cullmann, a New Testament scholar of international repute. The belief in immortal souls that survive the death of the body, he persuasively showed, was a post-biblical development from the second and third centuries onwards, and reflected the increasing influence of the ideas of Socrates and Plato.

In early May, the Moderator declared that the matter was now *subjudice* and was not to be discussed publicly by me or by anybody else in the church. Being unaware of how busily some were planning to bring about my downfall, I felt reasonably calm and relaxed (apart from the unsettling events of Easter weekend), and fully enjoyed some of the humorous incidents. For example, in the Auckland Presbytery Bob Blaikie raised the issue of my title; he thought the term 'Principal', an honorific I was often publicly accorded, suggested that I wielded more authority than I actually possessed. He proposed that, since the Principal did no more than chair the meetings of the theological staff (then known as the Senatus), the title should be changed to 'Chairman'. One of my friends in the Presbytery wickedly responded, 'That is a good suggestion and I would like to second it. Then we shall have Chairman Geering and Chairman Mao.' And that was the end of that!

Another incident involved an elder of Knox Church in Dunedin who suffered a sudden fainting attack in the Octagon and was carried unconscious into the nearest shop for attention. It was a milliner's shop and, on regaining consciousness, he found himself surrounded by an array of colourful hats. He concluded that he was in heaven and astounded those seeking to help him by blurting out, 'Good God! Geering's wrong!'

When my former teacher and colleague Helmut Rex died in March, he left behind a finished manuscript on the topic of Jesus' resurrection. This was published a few months later as *Did Jesus Rise from the Dead?* His widow pointed out in her preface that it was in no way intended as an 'answer to Professor Geering', since most of it had been written before the controversy arose. Rex had produced a very scholarly piece of work which arrived at a position midway between mine and that of my accusers. On the one hand he said, 'The resurrection of Jesus is certainly not an historical event in the sense in which his crucifixion is'. On the other, he defended the historicity of the empty tomb, which on his own admission some scholars, going back as far as Wellhausen in the nineteenth century, had regarded as legendary. In my view Rex, like the author of *Who Moved the Stone?*, fell into the trap of assuming the historicity of the burial story. This is simply the beginning of the empty tomb story, and it is illogical to use one part of a report to prove the historicity of the other. I incline to the view that Mark's Gospel originally ended with the words, 'Truly this man was the Son of God!', and that Mark 15:40–16:8 is a unit and wholly legendary, perhaps added to the Gospel just as Mark 16:9–20 was added still later.

In late 1966, the Presbyterian Publications Committee had sought to promote informed discussion by inviting J. L. Wilson, a moderately conservative minister, to write or edit a book presenting the more traditional view on the resurrection of Jesus. This now appeared as a symposium of six essays, entitled *The Third Day He Rose Again*, and containing a foreword by the Moderator. The authors included Bob Blaikie, G. N. Stanton (a former student of mine, then pursuing doctoral studies at Cambridge), B. R. Harris (a former Rhodes Scholar and then Associate Professor of Classics at Auckland University) and two conservative theological lecturers in Australia (D. W. B. Robinson of Moore Theological College, Sydney and K. Runia of the Reformed Theological College, Geelong). One of the latter wrote:

'The emptiness of the tomb was the sine qua non of Jesus having been raised ... To claim to believe in the resurrection while holding that the bones of Jesus lie somewhere in Palestine ... is to deny the resurrection.'

This was a diametrical rejection of the statement by the theologian Gregor Smith that had triggered the original debate.

During the three months leading up to the Assembly, its officials received a deluge of correspondence – to which, of course, I was not privy, but of which I received hints. Further, it so happened that in 1967 the Clerk of Assembly, Stan Read, was also the Moderator (the only year in the history of the church when this was so). Therefore, in giving advice to those preparing to lay charges of doctrinal error against me, he was often doing his best to remain neutral while wearing two very different hats. Further, he felt ambivalent on the issue itself, for like many other liberals at the time he sympathised with me but felt I had gone too far.

At one point, as I later discovered, Read privately recruited E. R. E. (Eric) Ross, Assistant Clerk and acting lecturer in Church History with me at Knox, to sound me out on how I would react if the hearing of charges against me were to be carried out in private, to avoid the adverse publicity it would otherwise bring to the church. This suggestion I unequivocally rejected, saying, 'I have nothing to hide and, having been subjected to widespread criticism in public, I insist on defending myself in public'.

Clearly, Read faced two difficulties. The first was that, under normal church procedure, any complaints about a minister's statements should be heard within a presbytery, thus leaving the Assembly to serve as a Court of Appeal. But the Dunedin Presbytery to which I belonged had already indicated its confidence in me and had no wish to lay charges. The complaints were coming from people in the Auckland Presbytery, which was becoming the centre for Christian conservatism, while liberal thought was being more readily accepted in the south. (Incidentally, this polarisation ran directly counter to the common perception of Auckland as the centre of the *avant-garde* and the south as living in the past.) Because the Theological Hall of which I was Principal served the whole church rather than one presbytery, I had no hesitation in allowing my case to be dealt with by the Assembly, even though this entailed surrendering any right of appeal.

Read's second difficulty lay in the fact that charges were being pressed by two parties presenting distinctly different arguments. Bob Wardlaw was a fundamentalist and a theologically illiterate layman, who sincerely and passionately believed that what I had said could be quite clearly disproved by quoting the Bible. As chairman of the

NZAPL, he felt he could speak for the vast majority of lay people and was beginning to feel suspicious of the clergy, believing them to have become a closed shop.

Bob Blaikie, however, had considerable theological expertise. While not wanting to be associated with Wardlaw's blatant fundamentalism, he also distanced himself from the Westminster Fellowship, which was beginning to lend discreet assistance to the conservative cause. (Arthur Gunn, editor of the *Evangelical Presbyterian*, later confessed on television that he practically wrote Wardlaw's speech.) Blaikie was trying to avoid giving the impression that he was charging me with doctrinal error; but at the same time he wanted to challenge the Assembly to declare exactly where it stood on the issues that had been raised.

For this reason, the charges against me had to be laid separately. Wardlaw charged me with 'grave impropriety of conduct' in teaching doctrines contrary to the Bible and the Westminster Confession by denying: (1) the Christian doctrine of a transcendent Creator God, (2) 'the Holy Scripture as the revelation of God', (3) the deity and supernatural power of Christ, (4) that Christ had been raised from the dead, and (5) 'a life to come'.

Blaikie, by far the more astute and circumspect of the two, charged me with 'gravely disturbing the peace and unity of the church by making statements which appear to be contrary to the church's teaching'. After enumerating various examples, he requested that the Assembly determine whether I had denied the substance of faith and, if so, that I be censured or otherwise dealt with as the Assembly saw fit.

When it came time for the charges to be heard before the General Assembly, to be held in Christchurch, Elaine insisted on taking leave from work to accompany me and provide moral support. Her lifelong friend, Shirley White, lived at Mt Pleasant in Christchurch, and she and her husband Ian kindly invited us to stay at their home. It proved to be a restful haven from the stress of the Assembly. Elaine and Shirley were allotted VIP seats in the balcony for the entire proceeding.

The Moderator of the 1967 Assembly, E. G. (Paddy) Jansen, had served as a missionary in China and the New Hebrides (now Vanuatu), and somewhat ironically, as it turned out, gave a moderatorial address on the 'Renewal of the Church'. On Friday 3 November 1967, I was called to the bar of the Assembly to hear the charges set forth by my accusers. The air was charged with expectancy and a good deal of drama. More than a thousand people packed St Paul's Church and overflowed into the hall, as the lamps of the television crews created a surreal glow and increased the stifling heat. The *Auckland Star* noted that Wardlaw was presenting his charges 450 years to the day since Martin Luther nailed his ninety-five theses to the church door in Wittenberg. The *Christchurch Star* observed that a perfect halo hung briefly over the church, adding that it was not of supernatural origin but was caused by four Air Force Harvards practising for an air pageant.

It had been settled beforehand that my two accusers would be given forty-five minutes each to present their charges during the Friday session, and that on the following Monday I would be allotted ninety minutes to reply. But right at the outset, Wardlaw faced a procedural problem. He sought leave to distribute to the Assembly a copy of the lecture I had delivered at Canterbury University in April. This upset and embarrassed some members of the university who were present, for they had guaranteed the privacy of that occasion. The matter was quickly resolved when I raised no objection; as I said in my address later, I had intended to bring my copy of the lecture to help me in my defence, but had inadvertently left it at home. Indeed, I was glad that the Assembly would have the opportunity to read it, however odd it might seem that words that I considered vital to my defence, Bob Wardlaw regarded as evidence of my guilt.

Wardlaw and Blaikie addressed the Assembly in turn to elaborate on their respective charges, and members of the Assembly were given the opportunity to question them. The difference between my two accusers quickly became clear. While most members of the Assembly obviously felt little sympathy with Wardlaw because of his clumsy presentation, they were puzzled by Blaikie's failure to make clear what he intended to achieve. He said he did not wish to bring charges of heresy against me, and substantially agreed with me that the Westminster Confession could not function in the modern world as it was originally intended.

On the following Monday morning, as I took my seat in the front pew, an enormous bouquet of flowers arrived for me. I never found out who sent it, but guessed that it most likely came from students of Victoria University. Then, as I listened to the opening devotions, I could hardly believe my ears. The New Testament passage being solemnly intoned was the Transfiguration story, which contains the words, 'a cloud overshadowed them and a voice came out of the cloud, "This is my beloved son; listen to him"'. Elaine told me later that she almost laughed aloud when she heard it. It was one of a number of incidents in this very serious process that must have made 'God in his high heaven laugh'; but at the time it was no laughing matter either for me or for my accusers.

My address to the Assembly lasted an hour and a half, with a recess midway for morning tea. First, I disclaimed any responsibility for 'disturbing the peace of the church'. On the contrary, I maintained that since *shalom*, the Hebrew word for peace, literally means 'wholeness', I was endeavouring to restore wholeness or integrity to the faith that the church professed. I readily conceded that those of my statements which others complained of could not readily be squared with the church's standards when taken literally. But there was a reason for that: those standards were written in times when people's view of the world was very different from what it is today: 'The creeds … of past times no longer answer the questions that men of our day are asking and we can no longer fob them off with pat answers from former generations which are no longer relevant.'

I also fully conceded that the task of reinterpreting Christianity for today's world was difficult and dangerous, and could lead to errors. But whereas my accusers had claimed that theological teachers should stay strictly within the boundaries of orthodoxy, I argued that they should be in the vanguard of change, not leaving that challenging responsibility to the parish ministers while they formed a rearguard, tucked safely away in a theological college and out of touch with daily life.

What was becoming clear, I continued, was that the controversy represented a clash between two quite different ways of understanding the Christian faith. That outlined by Wardlaw and Blaikie and their many sympathisers described Christianity as a core of fixed beliefs. In strong contrast, I saw Christianity as a living and ever-changing path of faith being trodden by successive generations of Christians who, while drawing inspiration from their predecessors, took up the challenge to express that faith in terms relevant to the culture and age in which they lived. Therefore, I concluded:

'It is faith that man needs, not past doctrines. These latter only become, like the law, heavy burdens to be borne. Faith has no security, no fixed doctrines, no infallible church, no infallible Bible, no assured revelation. I hope my accusers, along with the whole church, will see their way clear to let go their hold on whatever words, doctrines, and dogmas of the past have given them security, and launch out into this world with the same insecure faith as marked the patriarchs and prophets, the apostles and reformers.'

As I finished there was a spontaneous burst of applause, swiftly quelled by the convener, W. A. Best, who had explained at the outset that there was to be no applause for any speaker. After members of the Assembly had been given the opportunity to ask me questions, Wardlaw, Blaikie and I were then allotted ten minutes each for a final reply.

After lunch, the Assembly engaged in vigorous debate for two hours. Much to my surprise (and that of my accusers, I imagine), members hardly referred to the various doctrinal issues that had been raised. Indeed, they seemed almost to take for granted that it would be inappropriate to judge me guilty of doctrinal error; they were more concerned with finding the best way of dealing with the issue from a pastoral perspective, with an eye to the good of the church. Almost without delay, Jack Bates introduced a resolution that began, 'The General Assembly dismisses the charges against the Principal of the Theological Hall and declares that it is persuaded of his Christian integrity and conviction'. Then J. S. (Stan) Murray, a former Moderator and the Overseas Missionary Secretary of the church, who had taken a leading role in trying to resolve the tension in the Auckland Presbytery, introduced a long, seven-clause amendment, which, while exonerating me, was largely in the form of a pastoral message.

The two hours were spent largely in debating the relative merits of the motion and its amendment. At last, fatigued by the emotional tension of the proceedings, the Assembly allowed the matter to be resolved more by accident than by design. Its immediate action was to pass a motion by a massive majority and on the voices alone: 'The Assembly judges that no doctrinal error has been established, dismisses the charges and declares the case closed'. Sitting quietly at the back of the church, I was greatly relieved, but much surprised to hear the Moderator next thank my accusers for their concern in bringing the charges, without making any mention of me. The following evening, after further debate, the Assembly accepted a rather hastily constructed Pastoral Letter that was to be read before all congregations. It expressed confidence in me as a minister and theological teacher, and also declared its appreciation of the faith and devotion of Mr Wardlaw and Mr Blaikie.

But although the Assembly had dismissed the charges, there was no easy way to heal the divisions that had now become public. Bob Wardlaw resigned from the church and started one of his own. A number of individuals transferred to other denominations. Nearly all the metropolitan newspapers devoted editorials to the subject, and the trial even rated a mention in *The Times* of London. The Catholic newspaper *Zealandia* was impressed by my defence and likened me to Luther, but ended (perhaps predictably) by asking, 'Where does this leave the Presbyterian church now that it has sold Christianity down the river?'

The *Sunday Times* declared that 'the Church in New Zealand has known nothing more exciting this century' and had now come of age. The *New Zealand Weekly News* commented:

'... the Geering affair is not over. The issues he raised can't be forgotten, many platitudes of belief are destroyed and people have been forced to see religion as a commitment to be questioned rather than a comfortable habit.'

It quoted a housewife present at the trial, who said, 'I've just heard my longest talk on religion and the only one I've been able to understand'. In the same issue, the Revd Ross Miller wrote, 'Nothing will ever be quite the same again'.

In many ways he was right. Nor was it ever again the same for me. Just thirty years after I embraced the Christian faith, 1967 marked the second religious turning point in my life. Along with many others, I had grown to regard the church as a holy society, different from other social institutions in that it manifested a special quality of communal life. I must confess to being considerably shocked to find that behind its customarily benign face it could harbour poisonous animosities and sheer hatred – and in the very people who claimed to be its most zealous guardians. It made me feel shame for the church; I was saddened by the recognition that, while it encompassed many fine and even noble people, the institution of the church was every bit as human as any other element of society.

THE BATTLE OF
THE BOOKS

The positive character of the Assembly's decision left me quite hopeful that the church would move forward into reformation mode. I noted with some satisfaction the judgement of the *Sunday Times* correspondent who had witnessed the Assembly:

'The real question which faced the Assembly was whether they would choose to live their faith in the context of the nineteenth, sixteenth or even the first century; or whether they would be prepared to come to grips with the real world of the twentieth century.'

He correctly saw, as so many others did not, that the real crux of the 'heresy trial' was not how to deal with an 'oddball theologian' (as Bob Wardlaw spoke of me), but whether or not Christianity could transform itself into a viable faith for the modern era. 'The Reformers now have the ball at their toes,' said the *Sunday Times*, 'but will the church be equal to the task?'

Some encouraging signs suggested that the church might indeed take a bold leap forward. For a few months I was kept busy accepting invitations to speak at both churches and secular organisations, and found myself being enthusiastically received. A good deal of healthy public discussion on the religious topics raised by the controversy continued through the next three years, as shown by the publication of many articles and frequent letters to the editor, many of which were strongly supportive of change.

In January 1968 John Chisholm, an elderly Presbyterian minister who was interviewed by the *Otago Daily Times* on his ninetieth birthday, reported that for years he had held virtually the same ideas as mine, and had even preached them in Knox Church, Invercargill, during the 1920s! Subsequently I heard numerous accounts of ministers whose sermons in the 1920s and 1930s had openly denied the historicity of the Virgin Birth. But if this was so in earlier times, why had such a furore erupted over one article and one sermon of mine as much as four decades later?

When I joined the church in the 1930s, liberal theology was dominant at Knox College, prevalent in many congregations, and widespread in the large and influential Bible Class movement.

Since my student days, however, the percentage of evangelicals and other conservatives in the ministry had actually been increasing (and it still is); by the 1960s they had gained sufficient strength to challenge liberalism. It was my bad fortune to have become Principal of the Theological Hall just at the time when the evangelicals were preparing to challenge the liberal ascendancy for the first time since the end of the nineteenth century.

As a result of the very public controversy that had surrounded me, I became an all too visible symbol of the liberalism that the evangelicals regarded as the work of the devil; I was now a marked man, and the conservatives were ready to pounce if I said anything they disagreed with. To be sure, the Assembly's decision had dealt them a temporary setback, but now they slowly recovered and regrouped. Worse yet, some of the liberal majority who had supported me began to back away, in the face of the recent dissension in the church. Indeed, at the administrative level, the church was so anxious to show pastoral concern for those who had been distressed or confused by the controversy that it completely neglected those on the fringes or even outside the church whose spiritual interests had been reawakened by the debate. And this despite its professed concern for evangelism. As a result, newcomers often felt so unwelcome in a church intent on defending its now outmoded doctrines that they drifted away, taking others with them. Although the trend did not become conspicuous for some years, this marked the beginning of a steady decline in the communicant membership of the Presbyterian Church, a decline I found myself being publicly blamed for.

In the meantime, the controversy was entering a new phase that one might call 'the battle of the books'. First to appear was *The Heresy Trial*, in which the Presbyterian Church published the charges laid against me by my accusers, their supporting addresses, my reply, the Assembly's decision and finally its Message to the Church. While this was intended simply to make public a full and objective account of the proceedings at the so-called 'trial', it gave the impression that the church's official position on theological issues had become rather fuzzy around the boundaries. To be sure, the 'Message to the Church' neither endorsed all that I had written or said, nor accepted my theological viewpoint as the only valid one; but it did declare its conviction that, in my endeavour to restate the Christian faith in modern terms, I had not stepped outside the bounds of reasonable liberty of thought or expression of doctrine. And this was much more than some could accept.

It especially alarmed many Anglicans, in view of their denomination's current negotiations for church union. Some two hundred of them, including a bishop and many clergy, signed an open letter to their Archbishop stating that the decision of the Presbyterian General Assembly would make it impossible for them to unite with such a church. As one who had long been a passionate supporter of church union and who was serving on the negotiating committee, I naturally felt very disheartened at being even indirectly a stumbling block to achieving union.

At the very time this stir was going on, my book *God in the New World* was launched in Auckland at a literary luncheon. This enabled me to inform a large gathering as to just why and how the book came to be written. I explained that many people in the pews did not seem to realise that what they sang about in their hymns on Sunday was out of kilter with what they took for granted in the secular world they inhabited from Monday to Saturday. What I had attempted to do in this book, therefore, was to bridge the widening gap between academic theology and popular Christian thought; this I did by describing the nature of the modern world, showing how it had emerged out of the Christendom of the past, and sketching what path the Christian faith might take in the twentieth century. This was also an opportunity for me to acknowledge publicly my debt to Elaine. The very helpful criticisms she had offered as I read the draft to her, chapter by chapter, rendered the book more comprehensible to a lay readership. Indeed, it was she who thought of the title.

My chapter on 'God' ended with these words:

'By God-talk we are pointing to the deepest reality we can encounter, to that which concerns us ultimately. But we do not know what that is. The God that is known is an idol. The God who can be defined is no God. It is of the essence of human existence that we live not by knowledge but by faith. It is by faith that we are led to fulfilment and our ultimate destiny, and God is the ground of our faith.'

The book's publication was followed by a flood of conflicting reviews in journals and newspapers. No doubt because of the notoriety I had gained before it was published, it received much more attention than it probably deserved. I was very willing to acknowledge and learn from a number of critical comments, chiefly in the area of ambiguities and generalisations. But I observed that those reviews that condemned the book differed so much in their opinions as to demonstrate what little religious consensus exists in the post-Christian world.

A striking example of this diversity was a page of the *Otago Daily Times* on which former Moderator Jack Bates claimed that my book 'explains the real nature of the Bible', while the editor of the Catholic *Tablet* wrote that 'this book sweeps away Christian belief'. Father Ian Sanders, Professor of Theology at the Catholic Holy Cross College, wrote a long and trenchant criticism in the *Tablet,* ending with the suggestion that the book would have been more appropriately titled 'Geering in Wonderland'.

Not all Catholics were quite so abrasive. Bernard Basset, a Jesuit priest and author, was visiting New Zealand at that time, and he rang me to congratulate me on my book. News of our meeting led to a television programme in which we entered into a very fruitful dialogue about the substance of our two books, his most recent one having the intriguing title *We Agnostics.* Although we by no means agreed on all theological issues, I found Basset to be an open-minded and delightful man with a great sense of humour. When I told him of my admiration for his fellow Jesuit, Teilhard de Chardin, he explained the thorough nature of Jesuit training over thirteen years – a period so long that it led to the Jesuit joke that ordination was a reward for a life well spent.

Rather different was the television programme a few weeks later in which my views were vigorously challenged by an Anglican vicar, R. J. Nicholson, one of the signatories to the open letter mentioned above. But although he questioned and attempted to refute a number of statements he found in *God in the New World,* I rather enjoyed the face-to-face encounter, for until then most of the debate had been conducted in print, a medium that keeps the participants too insulated from one another. And when Nicholson published his counter to my book a little later, entitling it *Empty Tomb or Empty Faith?*, the producer of the 'On Camera' programme invited us to a return bout. Once again it was a vigorous encounter, though carried through in a good spirit. As soon as the programme finished, a woman rang the television station to say that her son, home from school with an illness, was absolutely enthralled by it. If even the young could find a theological discussion so interesting, it is no wonder that the *New Zealand Herald* commented next day, 'This is the stuff that television is made of'. Alas, viewers get to see far too little of this kind of live television, then or now – and partly because the churches have been afraid to have their doctrines questioned in public.

The controversy that had preceded the publication of *God in the New World* ensured that it became a bestseller, and the publishers, Hodder & Stoughton, sent me a leather-bound copy in appreciation. When it was nominated for the James Wattie Book Awards, the publishers flew Elaine and me up to Auckland in October 1968 to wine and dine us before the ceremony, where I was surprised and delighted to receive an award.

In the meantime, Hodder & Stoughton had done a strange thing. Perhaps because they had originally been an evangelical publishing house, they decided, even before my book went on sale, to commission a response from a well-known conservative, E. M. Blaiklock, Professor of Classics at Auckland University. This duly appeared as *Layman's Answer: An Examination of the New Theology* and was also launched at a literary luncheon in Auckland. There the author claimed that 'the new theology menaces the very root and fabric of Christianity as no other force, assault from without or betrayal from within, has ever done'.

While the book was welcomed by all those who wished to see *God in the New World* refuted, it unfortunately reflected such a fundamentalist approach that it failed even to acknowledge the existence of the historical and theological problems that my book had attempted to answer. Strangely enough, and much to Blaiklock's disgust, I was invited by Les Gosling, the new editor of the *Outlook*, to write a review of the book for his journal, he having written the corresponding review of my book. Les and I had trained in the same year, served several years in adjacent parishes, and had remained friends even though he was a committed evangelical and a passionate opponent of church union. But he had received a good philosophical training at Victoria University and developed a critical mind. Many years later, near the end of his life, he confessed to me that he was at last beginning to appreciate the views I had championed for so long.

Although I tried to be as positive as I could in assessing Blaiklock's book (for I had long admired his skill with words), and could readily acknowledge that it would be welcomed by those who shared his assumptions, I had to say that it provided no answers for those who had penetrating questions to ask about Christianity. 'It is marred', I said, 'by that dogmatism which has done so much to bring Christian preaching into disrepute, a dogmatism that knows all the answers and will listen to no interjections.'

Indeed, this book did little to advance constructive dialogue in New Zealand, but it did have a humorous sequel. An American Baptist publisher, evidently impressed by Blaiklock's exposition, wanted to issue an American edition, but recognised that doing so would be pointless unless readers had the opportunity to read the book it claimed to rebut. Thus *God in the New World* came to be printed in the United States by a conservative publisher! I imagine few read it, but its publication was one of the many ironies produced by the controversy.

Then in 1969 another refutation of *God in the New World* appeared, this one written by a Marist priest, P. J. Gifford, and entitled *Professor Geering in Perspective*. Gifford said that my book 'abounds in gratuitous assumptions and glib half-truths', which he proceeded to identify one by one. This strategy, which had characterised many of the critical reviews, is a particularly easy way to denounce any book; its weakness often becomes evident only when the critic is challenged to write a systematic alternative.

An interesting sequel may well prove my point. Having accepted an invitation to South Africa in 1985 to lecture at Pietermaritzburg University, I was further invited to stop off at Harare on my return journey to give a lecture there. The man who invited me was none other than Father Gifford, who was then teaching at the University of Harare. On my arrival, he told me he had completely changed his theological position and now agreed with what I had been saying back in 1966–67!

I suspect it was primarily because I had now become a public figure that I was asked to contribute to a series of monographs designed for discussion by students in their final year at secondary school. Mine was entitled *God in the Twentieth Century*. Although only a dozen pages long, it offers a clear and concise record of how I was thinking about God at that time. Too few people, including even scholars, are aware of how greatly religious concepts and beliefs have changed and evolved over the centuries, and this was a point I wanted to get across. As the following précis illustrates, I was here sketching 'a history of God', something

Karen Armstrong was to do in great detail some twenty years later in her excellent book of that title.

I began by telling how the belief in gods began, then described how Israel arrived at monotheism, and finally showed the impact of science in undermining the concept of divine revelation, thus leaving god-belief as an open question in the twentieth century. What, then, are we to make of the term 'God' in the modern scientific age? This I attempted to answer in the following words:

'When a man, in full recognition of the secular world of thought, says he believes in God, he is saying that he recognizes in human existence meaning and purpose which are themselves not ephemeral but are of an eternal character. He is further saying that the various values which both interest him and lay a claim upon him are not simply and solely conventions of human origin but are the expression of something ultimate and eternal. All the things in human experience which have for him this ultimate character are linked together in a unity and the word "God" is a symbol of that unity which is infinite, intangible and eternal.'

I now regard this statement as a little clumsy and inadequate, but it shows how far I had moved from the traditional theism of a personal God. This is no doubt why, when the monograph was published, questions were raised in Parliament as to whether it should be permitted in schools. And yet, when

I delivered it the following year as a lecture to young theological students in Queensland – one of Australia's more conservative states – it was deemed quite acceptable.

It was certainly not acceptable to my accusers, however, and especially not to Bob Blaikie. All this time he had been working on his own critique of the so-called 'new theology', which was published in 1970 as *'Secular Christianity' and God Who Acts*. He made it clear that, although the impetus for his book had been the controversy in which we had both been involved, it was not aimed at me personally, but directed against the 'death of God' theologians among whom he thought I should be counted. It is ironic that I by no means saw myself in the 'death of God' camp when the controversy began, but eventually found myself close to that position (as the above quote shows) largely because of the need to analyse at greater depth the doctrines Blaikie had championed.

The contrast between our respective positions, which became more accentuated as time went on, is very clearly set out in Blaikie's book under the headings 'Secular Christian World-view' (in which there is no supernatural, no miracles, no revelation) and 'Biblical World-view' (in which God creates, controls nature, acts in history and performs miracles). The understanding of God that he insisted on defending is usually referred to as theism. Although he did not use this term, he implied in all he wrote that God was to be conceived as a supernatural being who thinks, plans and executes his will. Consequently, Blaikie had no difficulty in concluding that any secular version of Christianity (such as mine) was so total a departure from the biblical version that it was 'not a re-interpretation of Christianity but a substitute for it', and consisted of 'a whole system of radical doctrinal error'. In his view, it was an error far more serious than those of the ancient heretics, Marcion, Arius and Pelagius. It became the duty of the church, he proposed, to recognise the new theology for the falsehood it was, and to insist that its ministers be faithful to the biblical witness to the theistic God stipulated in their vows: 'the alternative being a betrayal of Christ and the Christian Faith'. Thus Blaikie's book became an apologia, an explanation of why he had charged me with doctrinal error, and why the Presbyterian Church should now vigorously pursue the matter further.

In the meantime, the 1968 Assembly had given Blaikie the assurances he sought by unanimously restating its fundamental doctrines in a way that avoided the uncertainty left by the message of the previous Assembly. Among other things, it declared that 'God raised Jesus Christ from the dead in triumph over sin and death to reign with the Father as Sovereign over all', and that 'beyond death God will raise the Christian to eternal life in direct and unshadowed fellowship with Himself and His people'.

All of this would have been perfectly at home in the sixteenth century, but it was utterly blind to the fact that in the twentieth century we had come to accept a very different view of the universe and of the human condition. While the Assembly's statement brought comfort and relief to many by reaffirming all the familiar terminology, it showed no evidence that the church was 'prepared to come to grips with the real world of the twentieth century', to use the words of the journalist quoted earlier. So when journalists asked for my response to the Assembly's decision, I declined to comment, not wishing to arouse further dissension. But what I *thought* was that ecclesiastical officialdom could not bring itself to engage in honest and creative thinking for fear of disturbing the peace of the church by upsetting the traditionalists. In particular, the faith community was unwilling to face up to the question I had posed at the very beginning: what can it *mean*, in the context of the world-view most of us share in the twentieth century, to say that 'God raised Jesus Christ from the dead in triumph over sin and death' and that 'beyond death God will raise the Christian to eternal life'?

Thus I set about writing another book, this one

focusing exclusively on the issues of resurrection and eternal life. I had not done so in my first book because I felt it necessary to explain the new kind of world in which we find ourselves living, and to sketch how Christianity had helped to bring this world into being. Then in 1970, while I was still at work on this second book, two new volumes appeared: *The Resurrection of Jesus of Nazareth* by Willi Marxsen and *Resurrection and the New Testament* by C. R. Evans. Both largely supported what I had proposed in the short article on resurrection that I had written for the general reader in 1966. I was now able to draw upon these, as well as many other books, for a more in-depth study of the resurrection of Jesus.

The resulting book consisted of two unequal components. Part I, 'The Collapse of an Old Tradition', started by raising the question of what 'resurrection' *means*. I showed how the traditional view of a bodily resurrection had shifted from the miraculous to the meaningless as people came to adopt the modern world-view. If Jesus had been raised physically, as traditionalists wished to affirm, either he would still be walking the earth (since in our space-time universe he could not have ascended into outer space), or his body must have undergone a transformation. The recognition of this by biblical scholars in the last few decades had, as I showed by quoting from their books, already forced many to conjecture such a transformation; and yet there was neither biblical warrant nor the slightest mention in past tradition to support such a transformation. Thus an increasing number of biblical scholars were arriving at the conclusion that the resurrection of Jesus could not be authenticated as a historical event involving the crucified body of Jesus.

This meant that the term 'resurrection' had to be understood in some other way, perhaps through a symbolic or poetical use of language. And this, of course, opened the way to an examination of the history and development of such non-literal usages, the project I undertook in Part II.

The concept of resurrection is an idiomatic or symbolic expression of hope that has had a long history. It originally sprang from observing the resurrection of spring growth after the death of winter. It was later applied to the resurrection of the people of Israel, as in Ezekiel's famous vision of the Valley of Dry Bones. Then, under the influence of Persian thought, it became associated with the myth of the Last Judgement at the end of time. Although the belief in a general resurrection to come was embraced by only a segment of the Jewish people, mainly the Pharisees, it was already being applied to the Jewish martyrs in the Maccabaean Revolt 150 years before the Christian era. Thus resurrection language was already in use before it came to be applied to Jesus after his crucifixion by the Romans. It had been used to express the hope that martyrdom was not in vain, and that was exactly what the disciples of Jesus sought to affirm about his death. This affirmation was later amplified by accounts of visions and the legend of a tomb found empty.

The book was published in 1971 as *Resurrection: A Symbol of Hope*. It did not receive as much attention as *God in the New World*, partly because by that time I no longer held a church appointment, and partly because the topic had ceased to be of great public interest.

That the reviews fell into three main groups was, I thought, in itself an interesting commentary on the religious character of our post-Christian society. First the journalists, who often skim books looking for startling, newsworthy items, produced articles with such headlines as 'Another savage attack on the traditional teachings of the church', and 'Professor Geering back into battle'.

The evangelicals and Roman Catholics, who found themselves quite unpersuaded by the arguments I had advanced, were anxious to defend the traditional view. A review in a British Catholic journal described the publication as 'a very silly book'. Canon Michael Green said in the *British Weekly* that although I wrote with 'erudition, sincerity and charm', it 'required far more credulity to believe Mr Geering's far-flung theories than to believe the witness of the New Testament writers'. Now Green had himself written a little book on the resurrection of Jesus, called *Man Alive!* The very title epitomises the way in which traditionalists had come to view the resurrection in modern times: it was a miracle whereby, for the first time in history, a dead man had come to life again, and this miracle had caused Christianity to burst into life. Taking quite the contrary stand, I had tried to show that resurrection had been in the air for quite some time before being seized upon to interpret the death of Jesus not as a tragedy but as a symbol of hope.

A third group of reviews took the book seriously; of these, some were critical and some very positive. One worthy of mention appeared in the *Times Literary Supplement*. While granting that the book was 'written with great ability and distinction and with many valuable things to say', the reviewer found a 'contradiction at the heart of it. How can a non-event be regarded as a symbol of hope? ... We are driven back on the need for an Easter event'. Alas, he had entirely missed the point. There *was* an event – it was the tragic death of Jesus on the cross. The symbolic language of resurrection was what the early Christians used in order to interpret that dire event in a positive light.

Certainly I was disappointed that open-minded

and informed readers did not find the argument more persuasive at the time. Since the book concentrated on the issue that had sparked off the whole controversy, I judged it to be much better than my first book; it had more depth, and broke new ground by widening the historical context in which the idea of resurrection was to be understood. This was the last real clash in 'the battle of the books'; and by the time it was published and being reviewed I had already left the Theological Hall.

ABOUT THE AUTHOR

Lloyd Geering is New Zealand's best-known and most controversial commentator on theological issues. A Presbyterian minister, he is an Emeritus Professor of Victoria University of Wellington, where he taught for many years in the religious studies department. He was formerly Professor of Old Testament Studies and Principal of Knox College Theological Hall in Dunedin.

He is a Companion of the British Empire and in 2001 was named a Principal Companion of the New Zealand Order of Merit, which was re-designated in 2009 to that of Knight Grand Companion of the New Zealand Order of Merit. In 2007 he was admitted to the Order of New Zealand.

Lloyd Geering's autobiography, *Wrestling with God*, was published by Bridget Williams Books in association with Craig Potton in 2006. His other books include *Christianity without God* (2002), *Such Is Life* (2010) and *From the Big Bang to God* (2013). *The Lloyd Geering Reader*, edited by Paul Morris and Mike Grimshaw, was published by Victoria University Press in 2007.

About BWB Texts

BWB Texts are short books on big subjects: succinct narratives spanning history, memoir, contemporary issues, science and more from great New Zealand writers. All BWB Texts are available digitally, with selected works also in paperback. New Texts are published monthly – please visit www.bwb.co.nz to see the latest releases.

BWB Texts include:

Paul Callaghan: Luminous Moments
Foreword by Catherine Callaghan

Creeks and Kitchens: A Childhood Memoir
Maurice Gee

Report from Christchurch
Rebecca Macfie

'I think ... I am going to die.': Katherine Mansfield at Fontainebleau
Kathleen Jones

Hidden Agendas: What We Need to Know about the TPPA
Jane Kelsey